51 APPS
THAT CHANGED THE
WORLD

Whether its ordering food, hiring a cab, watching a movie on the phone, meeting new friends, taking notes or checking each other's social media, Apps have literally changed our life, Are you ready to know the amazing people and the fabulous stories that inspired these apps?

In this special book we look at some amazing stories and facts behind how these billion dollar companies started and the ideas their founders had which made them bilionaires.

We also look at revenue's and mindblowing statistics about money and growth that will inspire the Entrepreneur inside you to make the next billion dollar Company.

© Swimore Arkzenn. All Rights Reserved. No Part of this Publication must be reproduced, distributed or transmitted by any form or by any means without prior written permission of the publisher. Images used in this book are under the wikimedia Commons License and are the property of their respective owners.

TABLE OF CONTENTS

FACEBOOK	1
WHATSAPP	2
UBER	3
SPOTIFY	4
TWITTER	5
NETFLIX	6
INSTAGRAM	7
SNAPCHAT	8
REDDIT	9
TINDER	10
AIRBNB	11
ANGRY BIRDS	12
ZOOM	13
G-MAPS	14
PAYPAL	15
YOUTUBE	16
DROPBOX	17
YELP	18
TRUECALLER	19
QUORA	20
VENMO	21
PINTEREST	22
ROBINHOOD	23
TUMBLR	24
POSTMATES	25
VIBER	26
INSTACART	27
KIK	28
FLIPBOARD	29
EVERNOTE	30
POKEMON GO	31
MEDIUM	32
SLACK	33
TELEGRAM	34
WISH	35
SQUARE	36
CALM	37
FLICKR	38
VIMEO	39
GMAIL	40
CANDY CRUSH	41
G - CHROME	42
LINKEDIN	43
SKYPE	44
PERISCOPE	45
BYJUS	46
CLASH OF CLANS	47
CASHAPP	48
LYFT	49
TIKTOK	50
DISCORD	51

FACEBOOK
Started: 2004

Mark Zuckerburg started facebook in his harvard dorm room along with Eduardo Saverin, Andrew mccollum, Dustin Moskivitz and Chris Hughes to initially build a community of college students.

The company grew so quickly that by the time 2010 came it had over 500 million users and its value was determined to be at $41 Billion.

As of 2020 Facebook is one of the biggest companies in the world employing 40, 000 people. More than 300 million images are uploaded on fb everyday and it has more that 1.84 billion users every month.

The Company in the past few year's went on a shopping spree and aquired Instagram, Whatsapp, Oculus VR and many more for billions of dollars. Facebook Inc's Revenue last year was $ 70 Billion.

WHATSAPP
Started: 2009

Jan Koum and Brain Acton started Whatsapp as they noted that there wasn't a good messaging service which showed the users status. They were both former employees of Yahoo and applied a job at Facebook but were rejected after which they started whatsapp and the rest is history.

They released the first vesrion in 2009 and koum named it whatsapp as a reference to whatsap up.

Once they fixed all the bugs and issue's they released whatsapp 2.0 and the users grew to 250,000.

By 2011 whatsapp was in apple app store top 20 apps and by 2014 it had more that 400 million users which indicated that this messaging platform had just exploded in popularity.

Facebook quickly noticed the growth and bought Whatsapp for a staggering $19 billion making the founders instant billionare's. As of 2020 whatsapp has more than 2 billion users.

UBER
Started: 2009

Garett Camp and Travis Kalanick(Both Computer Programmers) started uber after a conversation in paris in which they realized that the cost of hiring a private taxi was extremely high and thus wanted to start a company where the users can use their phones to book cheap ride hailing services.

The App originaly allowed the users to book only black luxury vehicles

By the time 2012 came they had expanded into New York, Chicago, Paris and other countries where it saw unprecedented response and the users grew by millions overnight making uber an essential part of everyones daily life.

Today Uber is among the top companies in the world with presence in more than 65 countries and 14 million trips are completed everyday through its app. The company is valued at over $80 Billion.

SPOTIFY
Started: 2006

Daniel EK and Martin Lorentzon launch Spotify in Stockholm sweden as an invite only app.

In 2008 spotify is launced in UK, France and Spain but still is an Invite only app but offers users Free but limited features.

Spotify has seen immense user growth , with only one million users in 2011 to over 100 million paid users in 2020.

More than 40, 000 songs are added to spotify every day.

Has over 3 Billion Playlists to listen from. Ed sheeran's 'shape of you' generated 2.5 billion streams in its first month.

Spotify has paid over $8 Billion to the Music Industry. Spotify generated a record Profit of $511 Million in the first quarter of 2020. The company is valued at over $21 Billion.

TWITTER
Started: 2006

Twittter was started after a day long brainstorming session in which Jack dorsey suggested an idea where sms can be used to communicate with a large group of people and their current status can be shared.

The first known use of a hashtag first debuts on twitter on 2007 when it had 60, 000 users.

Twitter saw growth day after day and hit 200 million monthly active users by 2012.

As of 2020 twitter has 400 million active users and 500 million tweets are sent everyday.

Twitter reported a revenue of $807 Million in the first quarter of 2020 and has a valuation of $4.5 billion.

NETFLIX
Started: 1997

Started by Marc Randolph and Reed Hastings as an online DVD Rental Service.

Users chose the movie and recieved it by post and after they were done they simply mailed it back to them.

In 2000 Netflix approached Blockbuster (their Rival) for a partnership but were laughed upon.

By 2002 Netflix had 60,000 members and in 2010 they launched their streaming service and by 2016 Netflix was available worldwide.

15 percent of entire internet's bandwidth is consumed by Netflix, it has 150 million subscribers and has 14,000 shows and movies.

Netflix spent $12 Billion in 2019 to produce original content and saw a revenue of $ 20 Billion in 2019. It is valued at $184 Billion.

INSTAGRAM
Started: 2010

Initially named 'Burbn' by Kevin Systrom and Mike Krieger in San francisco as a check in app similar to foursquare but was later rebranded to 'Instagram' to focus on photo and Video Sharing.

The App grew in popularity and had 25,000 users the day it released and hit one million downloads in just 2 months.

By 2012 Instagram has 80 Million users and by 2020 it has over a Billion users and 95 million Photos and videos are posted everyday.

Facebook quickly noticed the rise of this app and bought it for $1 Billion cash and stocks, what a steal as Instagram today is worth $100 Billion.

SNAPCHAT
Started: 2011

Created by Evan Spiegel, Bobby Murphy and Reggie Brown who were both stanford college students, The idea was to create a social media platform where the images and messages dissapear after a while.

Within a year snapchat exploded among the young crowd and saw 20 million photos being shared everyday and by the time 2016 came it boasted 10 billion daily views which is a crazy number.

Users engage on snapchat like no other app and has over 210 million current users and 2.1 million snaps are sent every second.

Advertisers prefer snapchat as conversions are extremely high and can leverage features like face filters etc. All this makes snapchat's value more than $24 Billion.

REDDIT
Started: 2005

Started by Steve Huffman and Alex Ohanion when they were college roommates, they basically wanted to create the front page of the Internet and were accepted to Y combinator and later merged with Aaron Swartz's Infogami to become Reddit.

The Company became popular as users were able to particiapte in individual communities and express their opinions.

Over 150 million pages are viewed everyday and 500 million people use reddit every month.

There are 1.2 millon subreddits and it is the 7th most visited website in the world.

Over 800 employees work in the company and the company is valued at $3.5 Billion, Interestingly Reddit never spent more than $500 to promote itself in all of its existence.

TINDER
Started: 2012

Founded by Sean Rad, Jonathan Badeen, Justin Mateen, Dinesh Moorjani, Whitney Wolfe Herd Arun Gopan and Joe Munoz to basically ease thhe stress of meeting new people and finding new friends.

By 2014 Tinder had gotten so popular thanks to college campuses that it generated one billion swipes per day and matched 12 million people on a daily basis.

It has become the top dating app and boasts 50 million users and 6 million paid users a month and has made 20 billion matches since its inception.

Tinder reported a revenue of $1.1 Billion as of 2019 which values the company at $10 Billion, Pretty Impressive for an app that lets you swipe left or Right on a person and match you according to your preferences.

AIRBNB
Started: 2008

Started by Brian Cheskiy, Joe Gebbia and Nathan Blecharzyck after they came up with an idea of putting a mattress in their home and making it a bed and breakfast. Airbedandbreakfast.com was offically launched in 2008.

By 2009 they had over 10,000 users and shortly after in 2012 the company anounced they had surpassed 10 million bookings.

The company which owns no real estate and acts as a mediator has over 4.5 million listing on its site from over 81,000 cities, 200 guests check in to an Airbnb every minute.

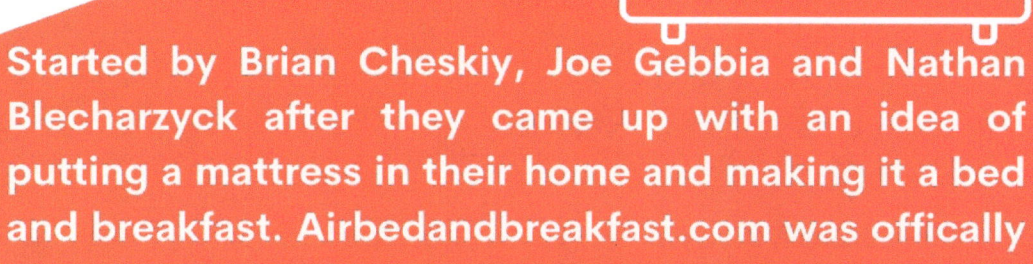

Airbnb is a boon for home owners as they earned $41 billion through the company in the last 10 years, The company has been valued at over $31 billion.

ANGRY BIRDS
Started: 2009

In 2009 the team at Rovio started thinking about a new game and jaako lisalo(a senior developer) suggested the idea of angry birds that fly towards enemy pigs, shortly after the legendry game was in development.

By 2010 shortly after its release the app hit the No 1 spot on the app store and became the first app ever to hit 1 billion downloads and changed the face of mobile gaming forever.

The game has become so popular that rovio has released over 26 versions to the original game and has released 2 movies.

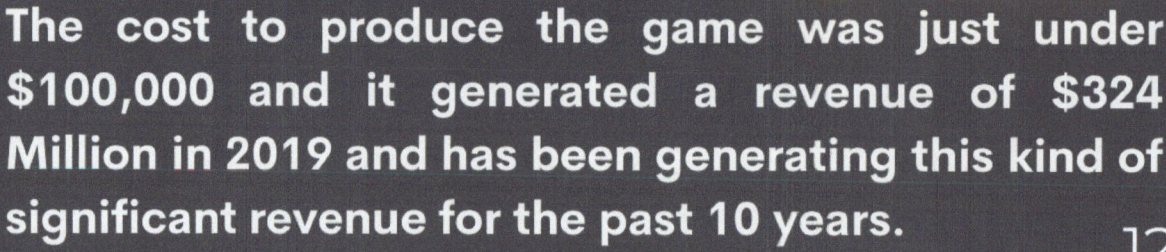

The cost to produce the game was just under $100,000 and it generated a revenue of $324 Million in 2019 and has been generating this kind of significant revenue for the past 10 years.

ZOOM
Started: 2011

Zoom was started by Eric Yuan who left Cisco Webex with 40 engineers to start a video tele confrencing service that was easy to use.

Zoom saw unprecedented growth in 2020 due to quarantine measures but had been around as a b2b video confrencing service and had 1 million users by 2013.

Zoom is popular among the masses due to ease of use and simplicity and hosts over 300 million meetings everyday.

Zoom has seen a year on year growth in revenue, being a publically traded company it saw a revenue of $328 million in last quarter of 2019 and expects a revenue of $500 million in the first quarter of 2020.

Google Map
Started: 2005

First started as a C++ Program by two brothers Lars and Jens Eilstrup Rasmussen which was acquired by Google in 2004 along with Keywhole and Zipdash and integrated with Google earth to become modern day Google maps.

Over the years google maps has become an essential part of everyday human life and has ammased over 21 million gigabytes of satellite, aerial and street level imagery.

It has over a billion monthly active users in over 220 countries and provides live traffic updates.

Google maps offers third party companies to use it's services and can customize it to their preference, this along with advertising google maps revenue is approximately $ 4.5 Billion.

PAYPAL
Started: 2005

It was started by Max Levchin, Peter Thiel, and Luke Nosek who initially were developing mobile security software and later merged with elon musk's x.com and became an online payment company.

Paypal is the most used payment processor as of now and is used by 250 million people in over 202 countries.

The growth can be accredited to being the first in the market and providing top notch safety and customer experience, It accepts 26 currencies and is active on 800,000 websites.

In 2002 ebay bought paypal for $1.5 Billion, today it employees over 80,000 people globally and reported a revenue of $18 billion in 2019.

YOUTUBE
Started: 2005

Started in 2005 when Steve Chen, Chad Hurley, and Jawed Karim could not find janet jackson's super bowl performance video online so decided to start a video sharing platform, they were all employees of paypal.

In one year youtube's success skyrocketed and it recieved 100 million views per day and reported that 65,000 videos are uploaded each day.

Today it has over 2 billion users and 1 billion hours of video is viewed everyday. In 2007 youtube started rolling out adverts which would totally change the business forever.

In just one year the three founders sold Youtube to google for $ 1.5 Billion in google stock, Youtube is a cash behemoth and generated $15 Billion Last year and paid hundreds of millions to its creators.

DROPBOX
Started: 2007

Founder Drew Houston kept forgetting his flash drive while he was a student in MIT thus he created a service where you could store your files on the internet, he was later joined by Arash Ferdowsi and they built Dropbox into a billion dollar company.

By 2009 Dropbox had a million users and in 2012 it crossed a milestone of 50 million users, the growth never stopped as today there are 500 million dropbox users.

As of today Dropbox has over 400 billion pieces of content which is more than an exabyte of data, wow. More than 50,000 developers have built their applications on top of Dropbox.

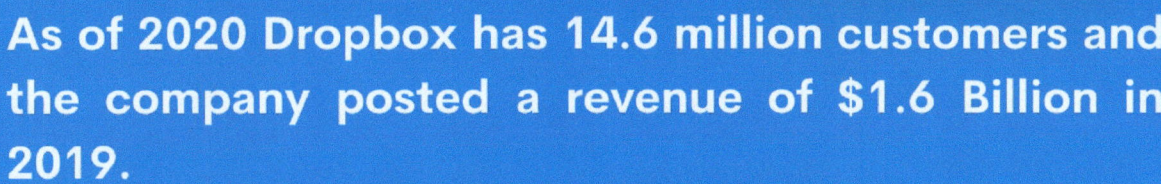

As of 2020 Dropbox has 14.6 million customers and the company posted a revenue of $1.6 Billion in 2019.

YELP
Started: 2004

Founded by Jeremy Stoppelman and Russel Simmons as an email based refferal network after stoppelman caught the flu, it was later redesigned as a crowd sourced review site and become an instant hit.

By 2006 the number of reviewers on the site grew to 100,000 and by the time 2007 came it had 17 million visitors and 4.5 million reviews and as of now it has 143 million visitors per month.

Yelp is extremely popular and is the 44th most visited website in the US and has 205 million reviews, these reviews can impact a local buisness and its revenue.

The company has aquired a lot of companies in the past and turned profitable around 2014, It posted a revenue of $1 Billion in 2019.

TRUECALLER
Started: 2009

Developed by True Software Scandinavia AB that was founded by Alan Mamedi and Nami Zarringhalam as a Caller Identification app.

The comapny grew slowly initially but steadily and had five million users by 2012 and a few years later in 2017 it crossed 200 million user mark.

The company actively blocks 460 million spam calls every month and has 200,000 new subscribers joining its service everyday.

With a projected growth to surpass more than 500 million users the company has started serving ads on its products and as of 2020 the company is valued at $ 1 Billlion.

QUORA
Started: 2009

Quora was started by Adam D'Angelo and Charlie Cheever who were ex facebook employees as a question and answer community which was to be better than yahoo answers and reddit.

By 2010 the company became popular among universities and students who posted and viewed the site soo much that quora was unable to handle the traffic.

As of today the company has 300 million monthly users who spend between 1 - 4 hrs on average on the site, the site has more than 20 million questions and answers to any topic you can think of.

Quora did not monetize their site until 2018 because they thought ads hinder with user experience and have recently started displaying ads, The company is valued at over $1 Billion.

venmo

VENMO
Started: 2009

Started by Andrew Kortina and Iqram Magdon-Ismail when they realized that traditional point of sale software was just not good ,they later concieved the idea for venmo when iqram forgot his wallet thus this mobile payment app was born.

Venmo quickly became popular among young students and college goers as it didnt charge a fee for transferring money.

As of today 52 million Americans use venmo and is accepted at over 2 million retailers across the state. More than 70% young Americans use Venmo.

Venmo was first aquired by Braintree for $26.2 Million and later Braintree was aquired by Paypal for $800 Million, today it accounts for 13 % of Paypal's dollar volume and processes over $100 billion in payments.

PINTEREST
Started: 2009

Founded by Ben Silbermann, Paul Sciarra and Evan Sharp as a visual catalogue of ideas that are arranged as pins and boards, its also known as a visual search engine.

In 10 months after its launch the site grew to 10,000 visitors and by the time 2011 came it had over 11 million visitors a week making it one of the top social network services.

Today Pinterest has over 200 Billion Pins and more than 340 million users visit it every month and is really popular among women shoppers.

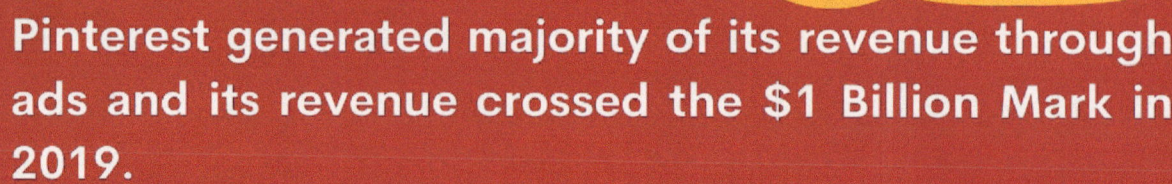

Pinterest generated majority of its revenue through ads and its revenue crossed the $1 Billion Mark in 2019.

ROBINHOOD
Started: 2013

Founded by Vladimir Tenev and Baiju Bhatt who realized that brokerages charged customers $5 to $10 per trade but it actually cost them fractions of a penny to do so thus wanted to provide access to financial markets to everyone not just the wealthy.

It quickly became popular as users could easily use their phones to invest in stocks, ETF's and cryptocurrency.

By 2016 Robinhood had 1 million users but it grew at a massive rate and had more than 10 million accounts in 2019 and boasts millions of dollars worth of transactions in a day.

The company is still seeing a high growth rate and has raised more than $500 Million Dollars in venture capital which values the company at over $8 Billion.

TUMBLR
Started: 2007

Started by David Karp and Marco Arment as David was interested in the concept of micro or short form blogs but since nobody had done it they both decided that they will launch Tumblr.

As soon as the service was launched they garnered over 75,000 users within a week and it went viral among the online community.

Today Tumblr is one of the most read sites with over 450 million blogs and more than 170 billion blog posts, They boast an impressive 380 million plus users a month but has not been able to turn huge profits.

In 2013 Yahoo announced that it would acquire Tumblr for $1.1 Billion in cash, Over the years Tumblr has lost its touch and its value has depreciated and in 2019 it was sold to Automattic for a much lesser value.

POSTMATES
Started: 2011

Postmates

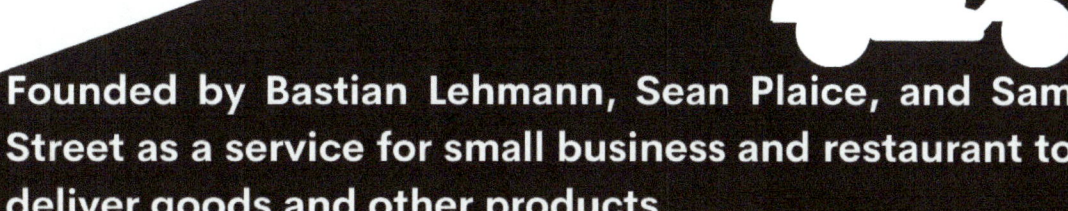

Founded by Bastian Lehmann, Sean Plaice, and Sam Street as a service for small business and restaurant to deliver goods and other products.

Any person could join as a courier which saw the company skyrocket its popularity and in 2014 it completed its one millionth delivery and had 6000 couriers.

Today postmates is active in over 3000 cities and delivers more than 5 million orders a month. The number of couries is a staggering 60,000 and 135 million people in the US use its app.

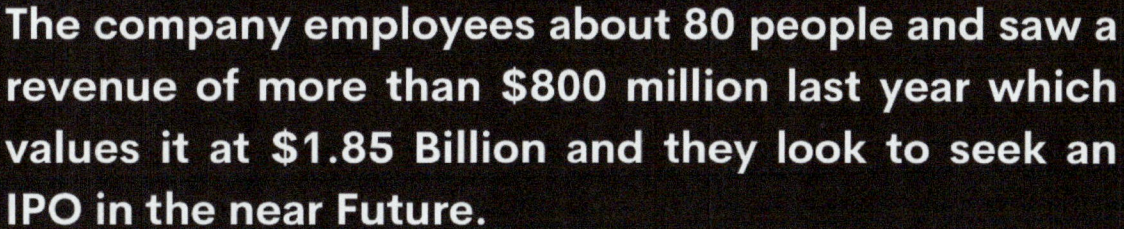

The company employees about 80 people and saw a revenue of more than $800 million last year which values it at $1.85 Billion and they look to seek an IPO in the near Future.

VIBER
Started: 2010

Founded by Igor Magazinnik and Talmon Marco who became friends when they were in the Israeli Army, they wanted to create an VOIP app that could perform instant calling and Contact Sync.

The app grew slowly and became extremely popular in the Russian and Ukraninan market where it had reached 50 million users in 2016 and grew steadily worldwide.

Viber is extremely popular in Eastern Europe and Russia and has overtaken whatsapp in some areas, Today the company has over 250 million monthly active users who use it for direct messaging and instant calls.

In 2014 Rakuten decided to Acquire Viber and purchased the company for $900 Million since then the growth has been steady and new monetization methods have been tried and tested which have been moderately successful.

INSTACART
Started: 2012

Founded by serial Entrpreneur Apoorva Mehta as a Grocery Delivery and Pickup service, Apoorva had started 20 companies before he hit the jackpot with Instacart.

The company became so popular among people that it attracted millions of users in just 2 years of its inception.

Today 30,000 stores use instacart and it is available to more than 50 million households, 250,000 active users use the app on a daily basis.

The company has seen massive growth since the last few years and reported a revenue of $690 Million in 2019 and is valued at $13 Billion.

KIK
Started: 2010

Created by Ted Livingston and a group of students in the University of waterloo as a new technology to be used on smartphones which later turned to be a messaging app that didnt need a phone number to register.

As soon as the app was released it hit one million registrations and saw increasing number of engagements.

The app is very popular among the young crowds and has 300 million users monthly and 6 billion emojis are sent everyday on the platform.

The company has seen increasing popularity and reports suggested that its revenue for the last year was $100 million and its valuation is $1 Billion, In 2019 Medialab acquired the company to expand its app portfolio.

FLIPBOARD
Started: 2010

Created by Mike Mccue and Evan Doll as a news aggregator app that presents it into a magazine format which is more easy to read and flip through.

Initially it was created for iPad and as soon as it hit the app store it climbed the charts with millions of downloads.

Today the app has over 500 million downloads and 150 million people use it to consume news every month from over 15 million magazines on the app.

The company has had multiple rounds of funding and has raised over $210 Million, according to reports the company generates between $30 - $70 Million in revenue a year and is looking for more products and services to offer to its users.

EVERNOTE
Started: 2000

Evernote corporation was started by stepan pachokov as a marketing software but in 2008 the company started focusing on evernote as a note taking and a task management app.

The users loved the app and it garnered over 11 million users by the time 2011 came around.

Today the app have over 220 million users and over 20,000 businesses use it, also the app has over 3 billion notes which people have taken since its inception.

Over the years the company's growth has slowed slightly due to new players in the market but nevertheless evernote according to reports has an annual revenue of $80 - $100 Million and is valued at $1 Billion.

POKEMON GO
Started: 2000

The game was published by Niantic in colaboration with the Pokemon Company, The concept was conceived as an april fools project with google called Google maps pokemon challenge and later became Pokemon Go.

The game was an instant hit and used augmented reality in which players could train and capture pokemons which appeared like they were in real life thus hitting 500 million downloads in a year.

The game today is played by over 75 million people a month who have captured more than 88 billion Pokemons and have collectively walked over 144 Billion steps to do so.

The game's revenue does not seem to stop as last year it had a revenue of $894 million and has a lifetime revenue of over $3 Billion and has always been in the top tier of the app charts.

MEDIUM
Started: 2012

Was founded by serial Entrpreneur Evan Williams who co founded blogger and Twitter in the Past, it was started as a website where people can publish posts or blog posts that are longer than 140 characters.

Medium grew at a nice rate with it having millions of readers within 2 years of its launch and by 2017 it had 60 million readers.

Medium allows the publishers to get paid for writing which has been quite popular, as of today medium has over a 100 million readers worldwide with over 400,000 paying customers and has more than 10 million posts on its website.

The company introduced a subscription model where some content is behind a paywall and users pay to read it which contributed to its estimated revenue of $ 70 - $100 Million Last year.

SLACK
Started: 2013

SLACK was actually an internal tool that the team of Tiny speck was using to develop a game known as glitch, Tiny Speck was headed by Flickr Founder Stewart Butterfield who is now the ceo of SLACK.

SLACK grew without any advertising at a blistering pace with it having 16,000 users in the first six months and over 2 million daily users in 2015.

Today SLACK is an extremely critical workplace tool used by over 12 million people daily out of which 6 million are paid customers.

The company is still to become profitable but reported a revenue of $201 Million in the first quarter of 2020 and is valued at over $20 Billion.

TELEGRAM
Started: 2013

Started by Nikolai and Pavel Durov as an instant chat messaging and Voice over IP app, The duo had Previously found VK which was a very popular Russian Social Network.

Within a few months of its launch telegram had 100,000 users and in just a year it reported that 35 million users use it on a monthly basis and 1 billion messages are sent everyday.

As of today telegram has over 400 million active users and 1.5 million users join the app everyday, it is the #1 app in more than 7 countries.

The company does not generate any revenue and wants to be free, However telegram launched its own cryptocurrency raising over $1.7 Billion from investors.

34

WISH
Started: 2010

Founded by Piotr Szulczewski a former google engineer in 2010 as Contextlogic, he roped in his college buddy Danny Zhang in 2011 to relaunch it as wish which lets users curate their wish list of products and buy it directly from merchants.

By 2013 wish had grown into a substantial e-commerce marketplace with thousands of orders daily and poised to become extremely popular in the coming years.

In 2018 wish became the most downloaded shopping app in the world and today it has over 600 million users that purchase from over 400 million products listed by more than 1 million merchants.

The company has become the third biggest e commerce marketplace in the USA and is valued at over $11.2 Billion.

SQUARE
Started: 2009

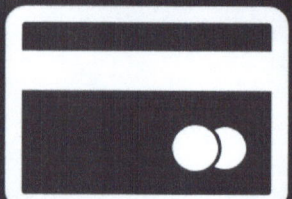

The idea of square which ia a company that makes software and hardware to accept payments easily by cards and other forms came to twitter founder jack dorsey when his co founder Jim Mckelvey could not accept a payment of $2000 due to not having a card reader.

The square reader became the company's first product that could attach itself to the 3.5 mm headphone jack and starbucks became the first company that agreed to use its services.

Today square is the primary choice of sellers and has over 2 million sellers who process over $10 Billion dollars in transactions in a busy quarter.

Square processes over $2 million dollars worth of transactions in a day and in 2019 had a revenue of $4.7 Billion.

CALM
Started: 2012

Founded by Michael acton smith and Alex tew as an app that provides mediatation, mindfulness and sleep stories and guidance.

The app grew in popularity as meditation became popular among adults and is now one of the top downloaded apps in health space.

Today the company has over 45 million downloads and more than a million paying customers.

The mindfulness app grossed $98 million last year and is now valued at approximately $1 Billion.

FLICKR
Started: 2004

Founded by Stewart Butterfield and Caterina Fake as an image and video hosting service, Flickr was initially a tool for a game they were working on when they decided that flickr has more potential.

Upon launch it became widely popular among bloggers and researchers who wanted to embed images on their blogs.

Today the company has over 90 million monthly users and over 10 billion images have been shared on flickr also everyday over a million images are shared on flickr.

The company was sold in 2005 to yahoo for approximately $22 Million dollars, Verizon acquired flickr when it purchased Yahoo, In 2018 Smugmug acquired flickr from verizon thus the company has changed quite a few hands.

VIMEO
Started: 2004

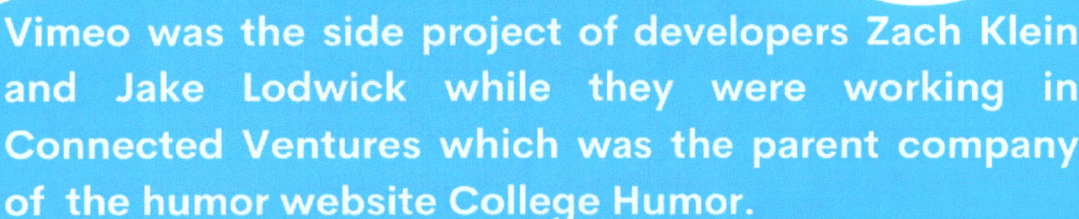

Vimeo was the side project of developers Zach Klein and Jake Lodwick while they were working in Connected Ventures which was the parent company of the humor website College Humor.

Vimeo was the first high definition and quality video hosting and sharing service that attracted a lot of brands as it tried to compete with youtube's free for all which allowed any content to be posted.

Today Vimeo has become very successful and has over 175 million monthy video viewers and more than 90 million registered users.

Vimeo's revenue grew year after year and has reported a revenue of over $180 Million the last year which makes the company worth over $1 Billion.

GMAIL
Started: 2004

Was started as a secret project by a google employee named Pual Buchheit , The tool was first used by google employees to access the comapny's internal mailbox.

Gmail was first offered as a beta service and then exited the beta stage in 2009 and had 425 million users of the service by 2012.

Today gmail is one of the very essential apps a person may use in a day and the numbers do back it up as it has over 1.8 billion users and more than 306 billion emails are sent on it everyday.

Google's gmail is a free to use platform but does run ads to keep it sustaneable and according to reports it generated over a Billion dollars in revenue the past year.

CANDY CRUSH
Started: 2012

KING was a popular browser game development company but in 2012 it decided to leverage facebook to create a game which used social interaction thus King's chief creative officer, Sebastian Knutsson suggested the idea of candy crush.

As soon as it was released it had been downloaded over 4 million times in just a week making it one of the top grossing apps in just a short span.

Today it is the top game in the app store and has players in all 7 continents and has been downloaded over 2.5 billion times. WOW.

Candy crush is a cash machine and has grossed over $5 billion in its lifetime and reports a yearly revenue of more than $100 million.

GOOGLE CHROME
Started: 2008

Eric shmidt who was the ceo of google back then opposed the idea of getting in the browser business but sergey brin and larry page hired a team led by sundar pichai to develop what we now know as the worlds most popular browser.

The browser was released to the public in 2008 via a comic book styled announcement that gained traction, over the years users started flocking to the browser as it provided better features and security.

Today it is the number 1 browser in the world and over 2 billion people have downloaded it and it has an incredible 60% plus market share.

Google has never released any official number related to google chrome but sundar pichai has been heard saying many times that google chrome is exceptionally profitable.

LINKEDIN
Started: 2002

Founded by Reid Hoffman , Allen Blue , Konstantin Guericke, Eric Ly, Jean-Luc Vaillant and other team members as an employement oriented online service where people can upload their resumes.

The new portal for job seekers and professionals was appreciated and in 2004 Linkedin had a million users and 2007 Linkedin hit a milestone of 10 million users.

Today it has over 675 million users and 30 million companies are present on it's platform.

Microsoft announced in 2016 that they would acquire Linkedin for $26.2 Billion , Linkedin has never looked back and has seen a steady growth in revenue year after year.

SKYPE
Started: 2003

Founded by Niklas Zennström and Janus Friis as a video chat and voice call appilication. They released the first beta version in 2003.

The desktop application grew in popularity as internet became more mainstream and in 2012 the iphone app for skype broke the record as it had 29 million simultaneous users.

Today it is used by over 40 million people daily and millions of companies use its business version, it has over 500 million monthly users and has over 1 billion downloads.

The company has been acquired quite a few times, it was first acquired by ebay for $2.5 Billion in cash and then acquired by Microsoft for $8.5 Billion in 2011.

PERISCOPE
Started: 2015

Founded by **Kayvon Beykpour** and **Joe Bernstein** when they realized that they could not show what was happening live in istanbul but could only read about it on twitter thus they started a video broadcasting app.

The same year it was launched it surpassed 10 million users in just 4 months and grew at a very fast rate.

Today it is a pretty popular live streaming app with over 10 million streams monthly and has more than 200 million streams on it till date.

The company was acquired by twitter even before it was publicaly launched , today while periscope is still popular facebook and instagram live are the leaders in this segment.

BYJUS
Started: 2011

Founded by Byju Raveendran who is a trained engineer, he first started teaching students so that they can pass maths exams, he later started Byjus the learning app.

The App become extremely Popular in India and was downloaded 2 million times by students in just under 4 months and the app was named the best self improvement app.

Today it is the world's most valued edtech company and has over 40 million downloads and more than 4 million paying subscribers, the student can learn from a number of topics.

The company generated over $100 million in revenue last year and is valued at more than $ 10 Billion.

CLASH OF CLANS
Started: 2012

The popular game was created by Game development company supercell, It took the team six months to develop the game and was based on old nintendo style games.

As soon as it was released it kind of blew up in terms of popularity and become one of the top 5 games on the app store.

Today the game has been downloaded over 500 million times and it has millions of daily users who spend significant amount of money to win at the game.

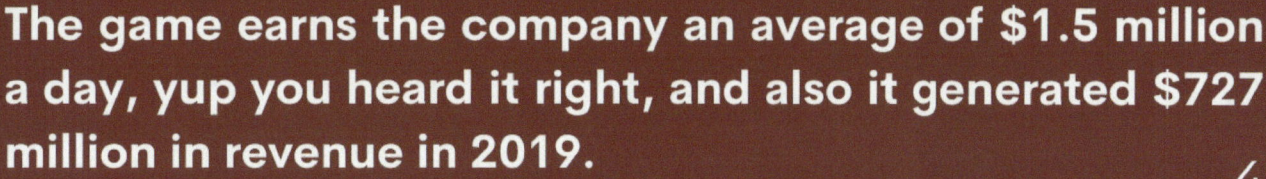

The game earns the company an average of $1.5 million a day, yup you heard it right, and also it generated $727 million in revenue in 2019.

Cashapp
Started: 2013

Developed by square, cashapp allows users to easily send and recieve money through its app and also introduced bitcoin trading.

The last few years saw ther rise of digital payments and cash app surely capitalized on it as it grew to 7 million users in 2017 and more than doubled it to 15 million in 2018.

Today it is america fastest growing payment app with 24 million users and it seems to grow 60% year on year.

Cash app generates a significant amount of revenue for square and generated $222 million in revenue for its cash services and $306 in bitcoin trading for the first quarter of 2020.

LYFT
Started: 2012

Founded by computer programmers Logan Green and John Zimmer as a service to their business zimride that was a long distance carpooling service. They used facebook to link passengers to Drivers.

The company competed with rivals uber in the short distance car share segment and was successfull as it completed its 160 millionth ride by 2017.

Today the company has over 25 million users worldwide and has completed 1 billion rides, it does an average of a million rides a day.

Lyft's revenue has grown at a steady rate and reported a revenue of $3.4 Billion the last year which values the company at $21 Billion.

TIKTOK
Started: 2016

Douyin was launched in china by bytedance and after seeing success the company merged with musical.ly and made tiktok available globally in 2017. Both Tiktok and Douyin run on different servers to comply with chinese restrictions.

The short video sharing app was made available in over 150 markets and was downloaded over 100 million times even before 2018 ended.

Today Tiktok is a behemoth with 800 million users worldwide and 1 billion daily video views, it has topped the app charts in almost every country with over 2 billion downloads.

In 2019 TikTok's revenue exploded and it made over $176 Million and the company Bytedance made a revenue of $17 Billion, Today Tiktok is valued at over $75 Billion.

DISCORD
Started: 2015

The idea for discord came to entrepreneur Jason Citron who realized how hard it was for people to discuss tactics in games using usual VOIP clients thus he wanted to create something more easier to use.

The App was well recieved by the gaming community and had over 11 million users in 2016 with a growth rate of a million users a month, the app hit over 90 million users in 2017.

Today discord is at the heart of the gaming community and has over 250 million users worldwide and over 25 billion messages are sent on its platform each month.

Being the biggest gaming chat community in the world its revenue was reported to be $91 million last year which makes the company worth more than $2 Billion.

www.ingramcontent.com/pod-product-compliance
Lightning Source LLC
Chambersburg PA
CBHW051217220526
45473CB00003B/1070